DO IT NOW!
TRICKS
RAD STUNTS & SNEAKY PRANKS

DO IT NOW!
TRICKS
RAD STUNTS & SNEAKY PRANKS

sarah hines stephens and bethany mann

weldon**owen**

contents

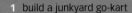

move

amaze

how to use this book

This is a brand-new type of book—one that uses pictures instead of words to show you how to do all sorts of activities. Sometimes, though, you may need a little extra info. In those cases, look to these symbols to help you out.

TOOLS The toolbar shows the ingredients you'll need to do most projects. Follow the steps to see the amount or measurement that you'll need of each ingredient.

makeup sponge

hairbrush   fake blood

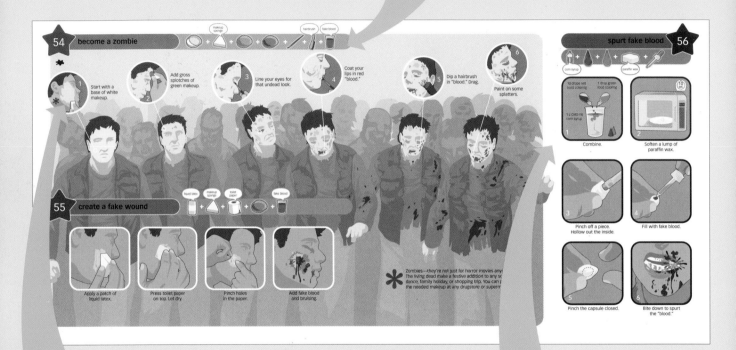

54 become a zombie

makeup sponge   hairbrush fake blood

1 Start with a base of white makeup.

2 Add gross splotches of green makeup.

3 Line your eyes for that undead look.

4 Coat your lips in red "blood."

5 Dip a hairbrush in "blood." Drag.

6 Paint on some splatters.

55 create a fake wound

liquid latex   makeup sponge   toilet paper   fake blood

Apply a patch of liquid latex.

Press toilet paper on top. Let dry.

Pinch holes in the paper.

Add fake blood and bruising.

Zombies—they're not just for horror movies any[...] The living dead make a festive addition to any s[...] dance, family holiday, or shopping trip. You can [...] the needed makeup at any drugstore or superm[...]

spurt fake blood 56

corn syrup   paraffin wax

1 10 drops red food coloring   1 drop green food coloring   1 c (240 ml) corn syrup — Combine.

2 Soften a lump of paraffin wax.

3 Pinch off a piece. Hollow out the inside.

4 Fill with fake blood.

5 Pinch the capsule closed.

6 Bite down to spurt the "blood."

ZOOMS These little circles, placed near or inside a larger frame, draw your attention to bonus information or important details about how to do a step—and sometimes how *not* to do a step.

MATH When measurements matter, they'll be written right in the box—like in recipes, or when an item needs to be an exact length. Angle icons show you how far to tilt.

3 c (700 g)   45°   40 in (100 cm)

a word to parents

The activities in this book are designed for children ages ten and older. While we have made every effort to ensure that the information in this book is accurate, reliable, and totally cool, please assess your own child's suitability for a particular activity before allowing him or her to attempt it, and provide adult supervision as appropriate. We disclaim all liability for any unintended, unforeseen, or improper application of the suggestions featured in this book. We will, however, be happy to accept the credit for increased awesomeness.

tool kit

Here are some basic items that you probably have at home, so they aren't listed in the toolbars. Pack a tool kit, and keep it handy!

scissors

glue

pen, pencil, and marker

plain paper

tape

utensils

water

containers

symbols

tell me more

Flip to the back of the book for extra info about this activity, including trivia, special techniques, history, or the science that makes it all happen.

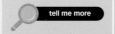
uses recyclables

This project helps you recycle old junk you probably have at your house. Go green!

messy

Wear old clothes, put down newspapers, and warn the parents. This one will be messy!

15 min

The timer shows the number of hours, minutes, or seconds you should spend doing a step.

Follow the little asterisk in a step to the larger one on the page for information about alternative methods or materials, or for tips.

move

Got a pile of random old boards and some wheels lying around? That's about all you need for a sweet DIY go-kart. Use the ideas here for inspiration!

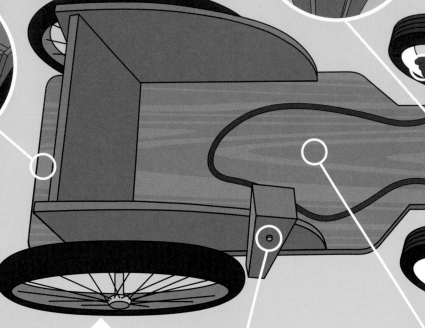

Connect the wheels to the body with a hinge. Bolt a crossbar between the hinges.

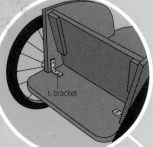

Brace the seat with wood and brackets.

L bracket

Scavenge two wheels on an axle.

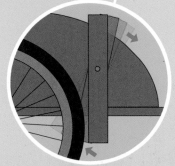

A piece of wood pivots to brake.

Brace the chassis with crossbeams.

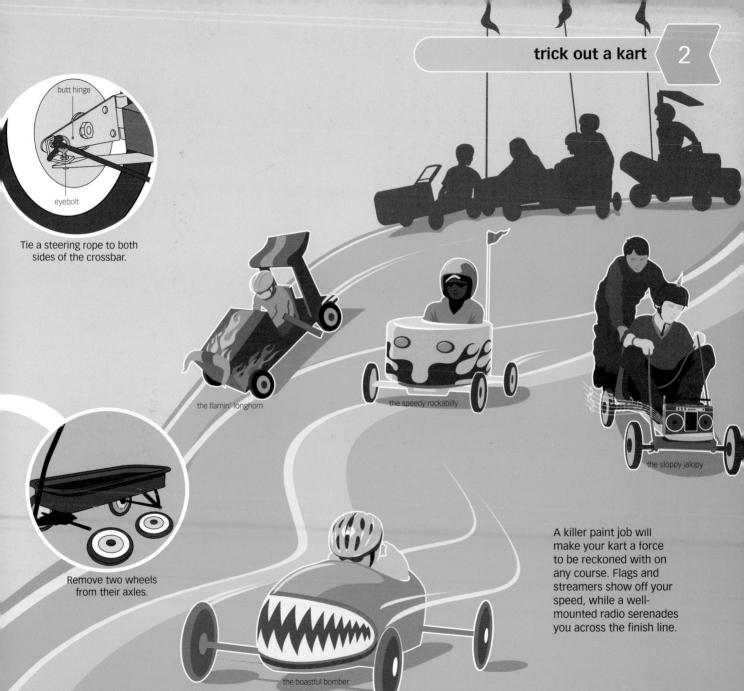

butt hinge

eyebolt

Tie a steering rope to both sides of the crossbar.

the flamin' longhorn

the speedy rockabilly

the sloppy jalopy

Remove two wheels from their axles.

A killer paint job will make your kart a force to be reckoned with on any course. Flags and streamers show off your speed, while a well-mounted radio serenades you across the finish line.

the boastful bomber

Push off to get rolling on one foot.

Extend your back leg in front of you.

Slide your front leg and torso to the side.

Glide with your knees shoulder-width apart.

1

Start with your feet parallel.

2

Push one leg in an arc to the side.

3

Pull your legs back together.

4

Repeat.

Push off and
crouch down.

Straighten up, pulling
the scooter with you.

Use your feet to flick
the deck sideways.

Tuck your legs as the
deck swings around.

Catch it with your
feet after a full turn.

Land, keeping your
knees bent.

1 Ollie up onto a ramp.

2 Straddle the back truck over the edge. Point the nose to the far side.

3 Grind down the ramp's edge. Ollie off.

1 Crouch with one foot at the center and one at the tail end.

2 Kick the tail down. Drag your front foot up the board.

3 Lift both knees toward your chest.

4 Land it!

4 Land it with both feet over the trucks (the wheel sets).

* When you're first learning to skateboard, ride on the grass with a parent watching. Always wear a helmet and wrist guards. With lots of practice, you can move up to the adventurous tricks shown here!

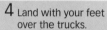

4 Land with your feet over the trucks.

3 Bring both feet above the board as it turns.

2 Leap. Kick the board into a sick spin.

1 Squat down to gather momentum.

1 Dive into a handstand. Grab the board on the outside of both trucks.

2 Bend your knees. Jerk the board to spin it.

3 Release it. Pull your legs under your hips.

4 Land with both feet over the trucks.

10 freeze an ice rink

Find a level spot and pack snow into walls.

Pour water over walls and let it freeze.

Lay down a tarp with plenty of overhang.

Add water and let it set for a few freezing nights.

11 skate a back crossover

Start skating backward. Gather momentum.

Cross your right foot in front of your left.

Bring your left foot to the side.

Repeat, starting with your right foot.

improvise a sled | 12

plastic trash
can lid

metal
baking tray

garbage bag

cardboard

cooking spray on
a shower curtain

dominate a snowball fight | 13

Seek the high ground and
use the element of surprise.

Stockpile ammo so you're
always ready to reload.

Many of the sled materials
can double as shields.

Form defensive walls and
keep your ammo mobile.

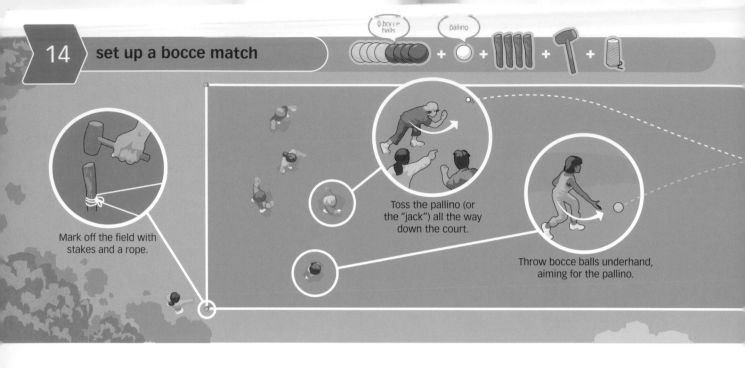

14 set up a bocce match

Mark off the field with stakes and a rope.

Toss the pallino (or the "jack") all the way down the court.

Throw bocce balls underhand, aiming for the pallino.

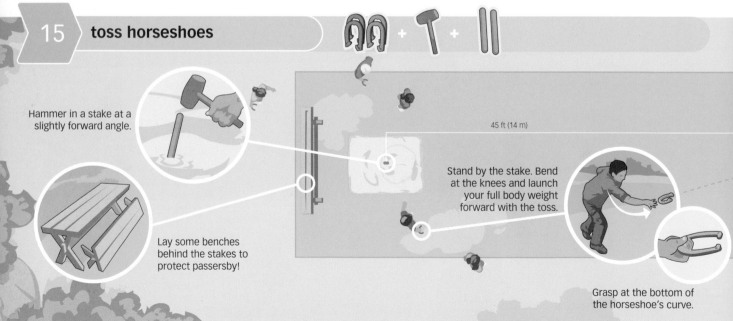

15 toss horseshoes

Hammer in a stake at a slightly forward angle.

Lay some benches behind the stakes to protect passersby!

45 ft (14 m)

Stand by the stake. Bend at the knees and launch your full body weight forward with the toss.

Grasp at the bottom of the horseshoe's curve.

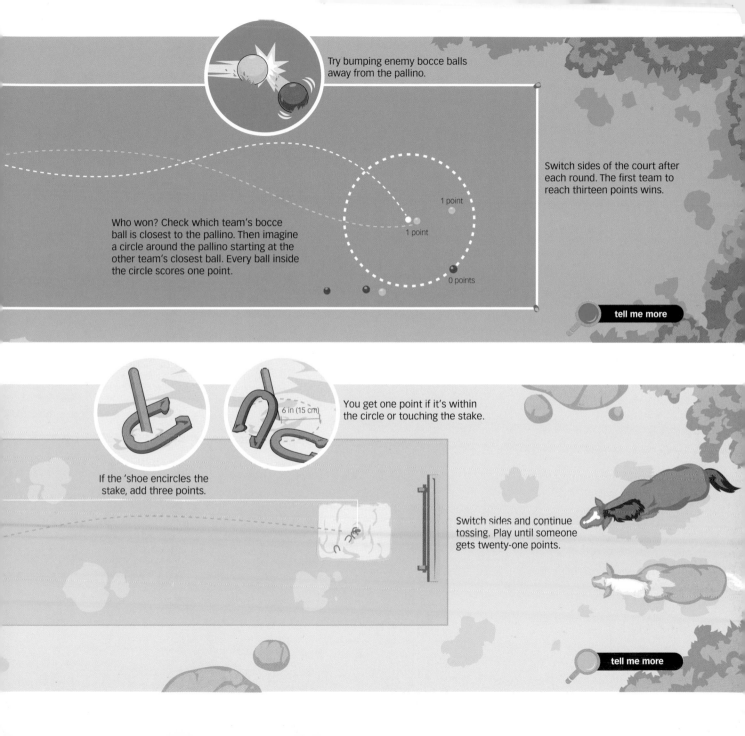

Try bumping enemy bocce balls away from the pallino.

Who won? Check which team's bocce ball is closest to the pallino. Then imagine a circle around the pallino starting at the other team's closest ball. Every ball inside the circle scores one point.

1 point

1 point

0 points

Switch sides of the court after each round. The first team to reach thirteen points wins.

tell me more

You get one point if it's within the circle or touching the stake.

6 in (15 cm)

If the 'shoe encircles the stake, add three points.

Switch sides and continue tossing. Play until someone gets twenty-one points.

tell me more

16 head a soccer ball

Hit the lower part of the ball to send it up.

Bend from the waist. Close your mouth and hit squarely.

Hit the top part of the ball to send it down.

17 master goalie moves

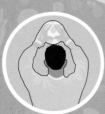
Make a diamond with your hands.

Start in the basic goalkeeper position.

Dive to make the catch.

Pull to your chest.

Scoop up the ball with both hands.

Hug the ball to your chest.

Cover the ball.

pitch a fastball 18

1 Put index and middle fingers on the seam.

2 Hide your hand to conceal your grip.

3 Shift to your back foot. Angle your front.

4 Wind up using your front leg and arm.

5 Release with your fingers over the ball.

6 Follow through after you throw.

sink a free throw 19

1 Stand at the free-throw line.

2 Crouch down. Keep your knees loose.

3 Focus on the backboard.

4 Put one hand on the ball's side to guide it.

5 Straighten up. Flick your wrists.

6 Swish!

ride a boogie board

1 Wear flippers for speed.

2 Swim past the wave break.

3 Watch for a perfect wave.

4 Swim hard in front of the wave.

21 bodysurf a wave

Swim out beyond the wave break.

Wait for a wave, then swim in front of it.

Swim to the side of the break.

Take a deep breath. Steer with your arms.

5 Use your hands and shoulders to steer.

6 Ride the curl!

Gnarly!

* Riding in the "curl" (perpendicular to the direction the wave is heading) takes practice! Start by riding the wave straight into the beach.

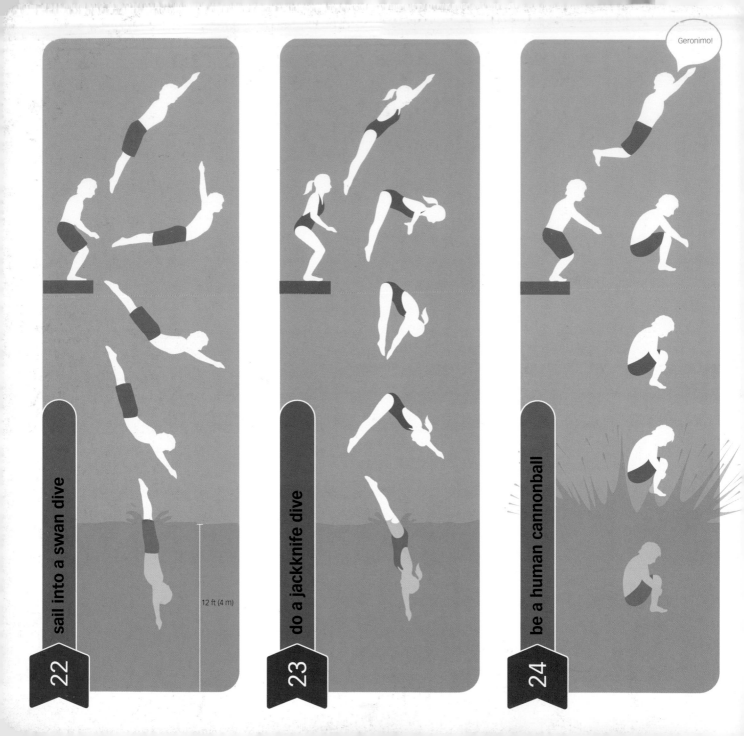

22 sail into a swan dive

12 ft (4 m)

23 do a jackknife dive

24 be a human cannonball

Geronimo!

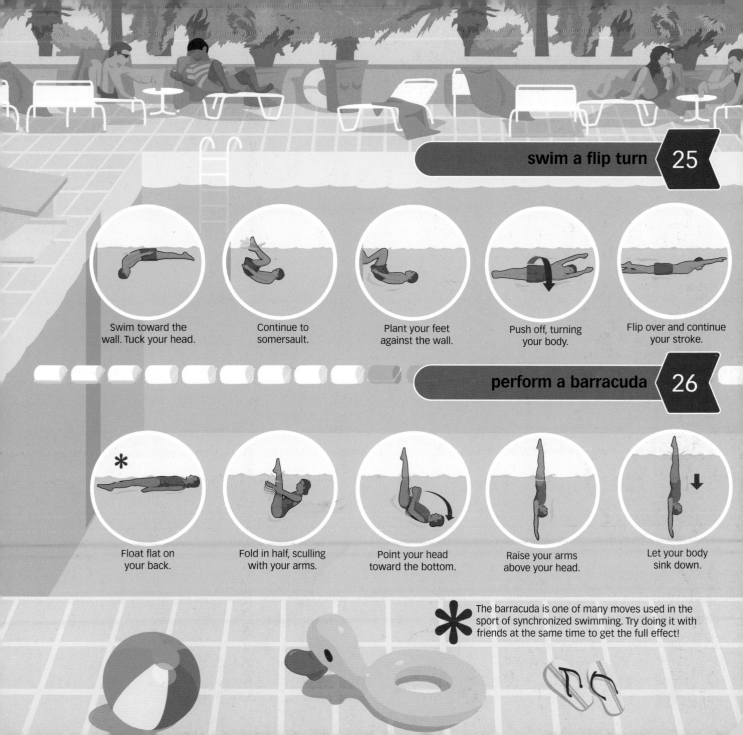

Swim toward the wall. Tuck your head.

Continue to somersault.

Plant your feet against the wall.

Push off, turning your body.

Flip over and continue your stroke.

perform a barracuda 26

* Float flat on your back.

Fold in half, sculling with your arms.

Point your head toward the bottom.

Raise your arms above your head.

Let your body sink down.

* The barracuda is one of many moves used in the sport of synchronized swimming. Try doing it with friends at the same time to get the full effect!

27 do the worm

Kick back to gather momentum.

Snap up, raising your hips off the floor.

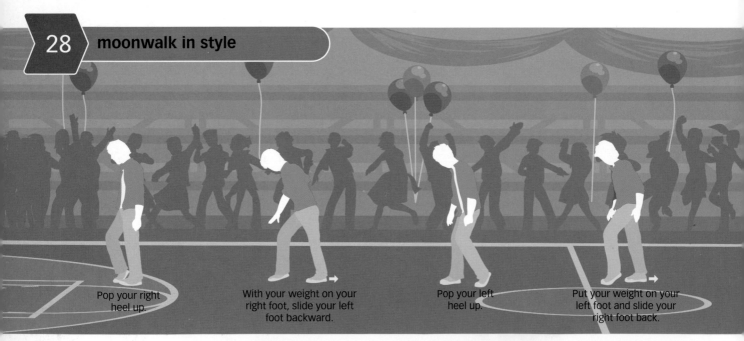

28 moonwalk in style

Pop your right heel up.

With your weight on your right foot, slide your left foot backward.

Pop your left heel up.

Put your weight on your left foot and slide your right foot back.

45°

Land on your toes
and push up.

Repeat, starting with
your right heel up.

Slide your left foot
back. You got it!

Pivot and . . .

. . . moonwalk back
the other way.

29 ❯ stand on your head

1

Clear away furniture.
Kneel down.

2

Put your head and
hands down.

3

Straighten your legs.

4

Set one knee on
your elbow.

5

Put the other knee
on the other elbow.

6

Raise both legs
into the air.

30 ❯ walk on your hands

1

Stand in an open,
flat area.

2

Dive forward. Kick
one foot in the air.

3

Kick off with your
other foot.

4

Swing both legs up.
Bend your knees.

5 ←

"Step" one
hand forward.

6 ←

Bring the other
hand forward.

Want to turn head over heels? Practice each phase until you've got it down, then move to the next. Take it slow!

1 Gently stretch into a bridge position.

2 "Walk" your hands down a wall into a bridge. Then try it without the wall.

3 Walk up the wall, then kick over.

4 Practice kicking over without the wall. Tighten your stomach muscles.

5 Put it all together, and tumble off into the distance.

Grab the bar. Bring your toes up to touch the bar.

Place your legs over the bar.

Hang from the bar by your knees.

Start swinging back and forth to build momentum.

When you're cruising for a perfect high bar, make sure there's a soft surface underneath. You'll also need a spotter to help you practice these moves—they're more fun with an audience anyway!

33 skin the cat

Seize the bar and kick back to build momentum.

Swing your legs up. Bring both under the bar.

Let your legs drop down.

Let go, and land with your knees bent.

Keep swinging—you want to have a lot of speed!

Release the bar by unbending your knees.

Tuck your legs underneath you.

Nail your landing with your knees bent.

*Start upright on the bar.

Keeping your arms locked, swing your legs back.

Sweep your legs around the bar in a circle.

Presto! You're right back where you started.

Crouch low.

Hop up, pulling the handlebars with you.

Point your toes down. Keep pulling up!

Tuck your legs up to raise the back wheel.

Land it!

※ Don't have a dirt-bike course nearby? Practice your tricks on the grass to avoid gnarly skinned knees. When you feel confident, move up to the pavement!

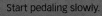

Start pedaling slowly.

Push one pedal down hard and lean backward.

Lean back farther and pull up on the handlebars.

Rock out! Keep your balance.

Lean forward and push the handlebars down.

Set the front wheel down.

drill   rubber tube   mulch

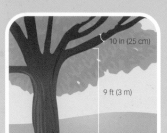

10 in (25 cm)

9 ft (3 m)

Start with a sturdy tree.

Clean an old tire.

Drill three holes
for drainage.

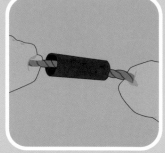

Add tubing to protect the
tree and prevent fraying.

Ask an adult to place
the rope.

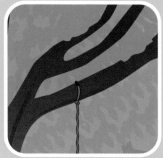

Have an adult tie the
rope securely.

Hang with the drainage
holes at the bottom.

Add some mulch for
softer landings.

Begin with a bow.

Hop nimbly through hoops.

Move like a cat on a ledge.

Practice your aim with a paper ninja star.

amaze

⭐ 40 shimmy up walls

Place one leg up. Wedge yourself between walls.

Bring up the other leg.

Straighten your arms to lift your torso. Step up.

⭐ 41 bounce off a wall

* Even the most fearless daredevil needs a soft landing sometimes. Start off doing these tricks over a mattress.

Run. Plan where to place your foot on the wall.

Put your right foot on the wall. Push off the ground.

Swing your left leg around, turning your body.

Push off the wall and land with your knees bent.

do a stuntman vault 42

Get a running start.

Plant your hand, then jump off the ground.

Swing your legs up and over.

Keep your knees loose as you land.

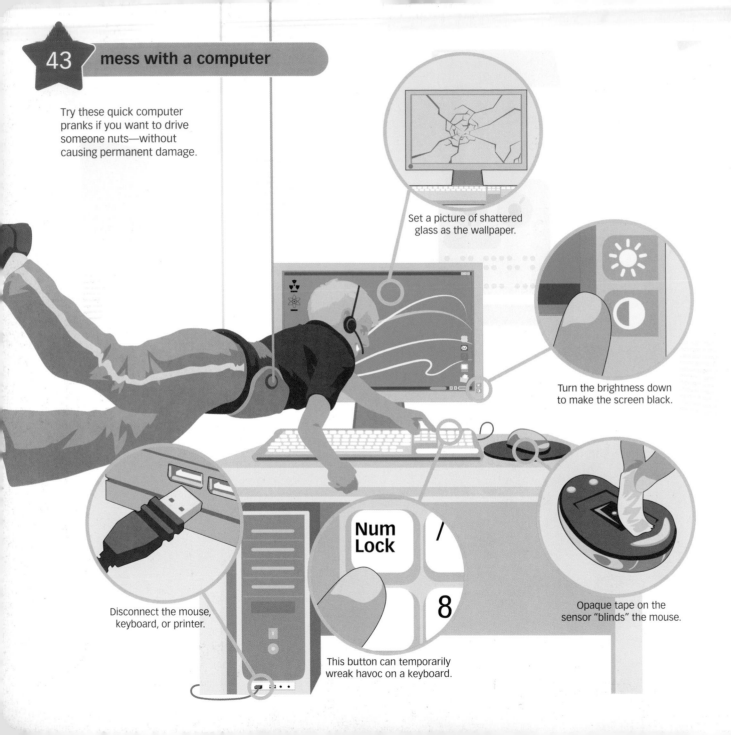

mess with a computer

Try these quick computer pranks if you want to drive someone nuts—without causing permanent damage.

Set a picture of shattered glass as the wallpaper.

Turn the brightness down to make the screen black.

Disconnect the mouse, keyboard, or printer.

Num Lock / 8

This button can temporarily wreak havoc on a keyboard.

Opaque tape on the sensor "blinds" the mouse.

Snap a pic while rotating to follow a moving object.

blurry-background action shot

Take a picture with your camera on the ground.

ant's-eye view

Have one person stand back and higher up than another.

tiny-friend illusion

form shadow puppets

alligator

bird

snake

boar

elephant

horse

standing dog

camel

llama

rabbit

human

deer

goat

turtle

Roll paper into a tube.

Tape.

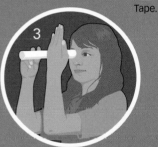

Hold the tube to your eye.
Put your hand next to it.

Keep both eyes open,
looking at a point in the
distance, past your palm.
You'll see right through
your hand!

Hold your fingers together
in front of your nose.

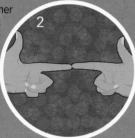

Look at your fingers.

Pull your fingers apart
and focus behind them.

Move your fingers together
and apart to change the size
of your tiny floating finger.

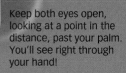

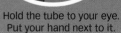

tell me more

build a creepy sarcophagus

butcher paper
+
+

1
2
3
4
5
6
7
8
9

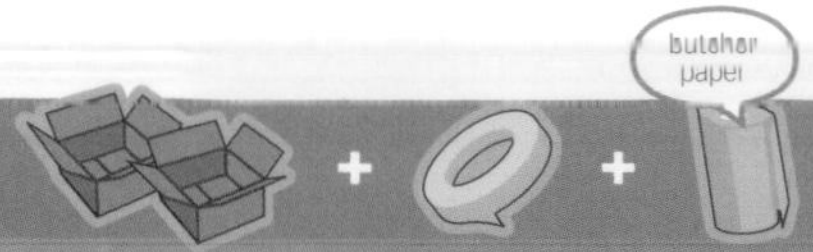

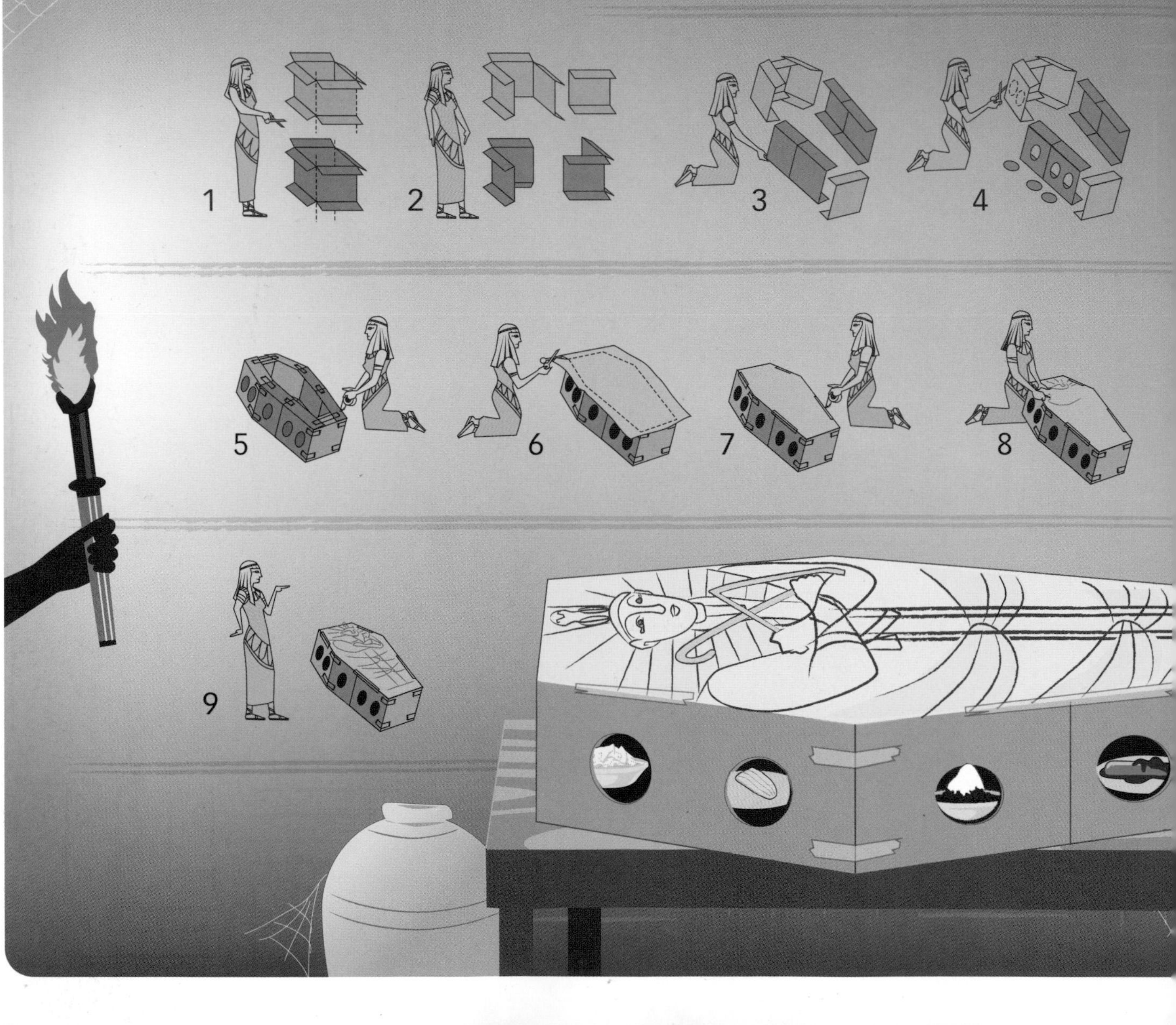

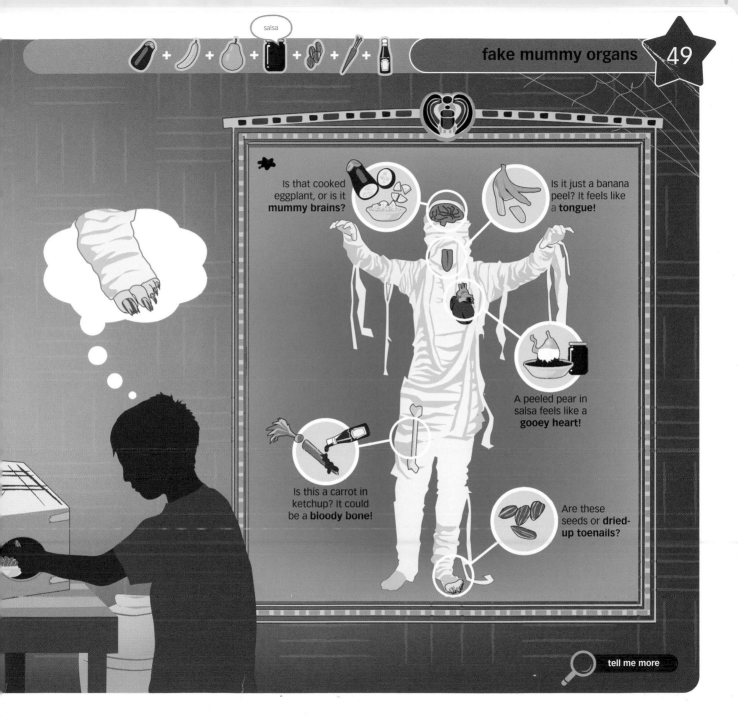

1 Make a torso with the chicken wire. Stuff it with newspaper, then cover with fake fur.

2 Cut features out of felt and glue on.

3 Decorate overalls to look like chicken legs.

4 Sew the torso to the overalls' back.

5 Stuff the pants and socks with newspaper. Sew the shoes to the socks, and the socks to the pants.

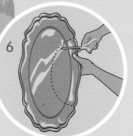

6 Cut out a space for your hips.

7 Glue the wings and pants to the platter.

8 Cut a slit up a jacket and shirt.

9 Put on the overalls, shirt, and jacket.

paint funny feet **51**

draw hand costumes **52**

create chin people **53**

Freak out friends and family alike with a
topsy-turvy version of yourself. Turn upside
down, and have a friend decorate your chin
to look like a face. Weird!

54 become a zombie

makeup sponge · hairbrush · fake blood

1. Start with a base of white makeup.
2. Add gross splotches of green makeup.
3. Line your eyes for that undead look.
4. Coat your lips in red "blood."

55 create a fake wound

liquid latex + makeup sponge + toilet paper + fake blood

- Apply a patch of liquid latex.
- Press toilet paper on top. Let dry.
- Pinch holes in the paper.
- Add fake blood and bruising.

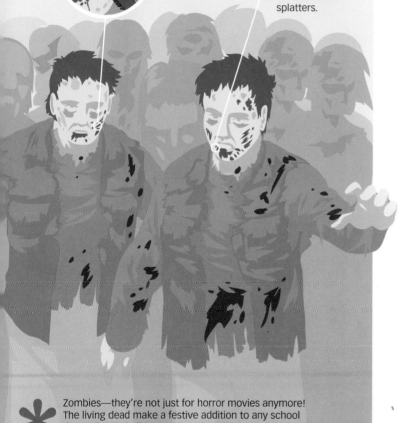

Dip a hairbrush in "blood." Drag.

Paint on some splatters.

Zombies—they're not just for horror movies anymore! The living dead make a festive addition to any school dance, family holiday, or shopping trip. You can pick up the needed makeup at any drugstore or supermarket.

corn syrup + + + paraffin wax +

10 drops red food coloring   1 drop green food coloring

1 c (240 ml) corn syrup

1

Combine.

10 sec

2

Soften a lump of paraffin wax.

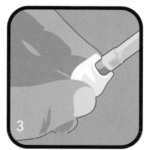

3

Pinch off a piece. Hollow out the inside.

4

Fill with fake blood.

5

Pinch the capsule closed.

6

Bite down to spurt the "blood."

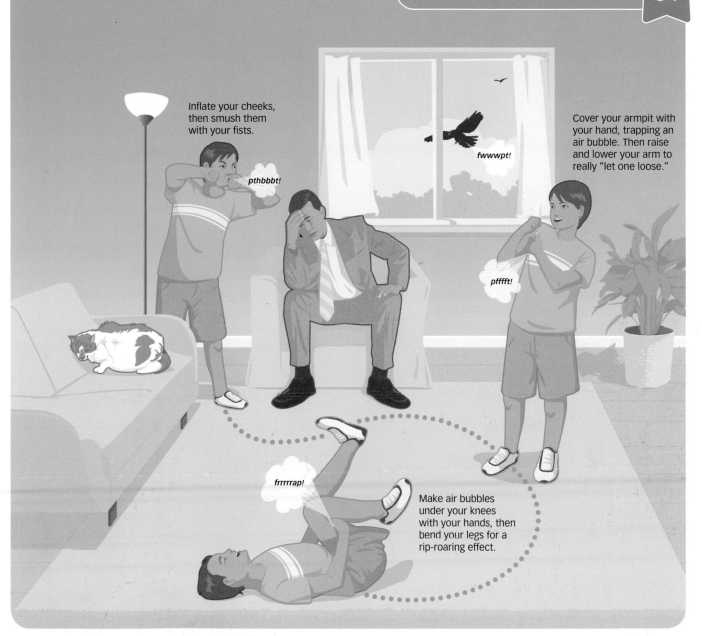

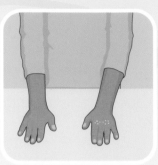

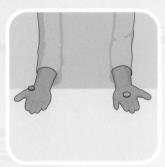

Put a coin on each palm, with one near your thumb.

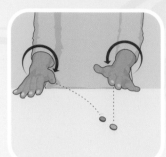

Flip your hands, shooting the coins under one hand.

The audience imagines there's a coin under each.

Turn the empty palm. Then reveal the missing coin!

63 bring a dove back to life

Cut a head from a fake dove; decorate to match.

Hide the fake head in your pocket.

Pet him. He's real!

Round up an audience. Show them the real dove.

Gently tuck the real dove's head. Put the fake over it.

Hang a string over
your palm.

Loop the back end over
your middle finger.

Slide the loop down
around your knuckles.

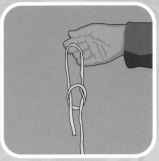

Pull the string between
your fingers up.

Pull the fake head
away suddenly.

Cover the real dove
with the fake head.

Tuck the fake; blow on the
dove to raise his head.

Release, putting the fake
head back in your pocket.

Stroll along casually.

Hook your back foot
behind your front foot.

"Trip" over your front foot,
landing on your knees.

Fall from your knees to your
hands, then to your face.

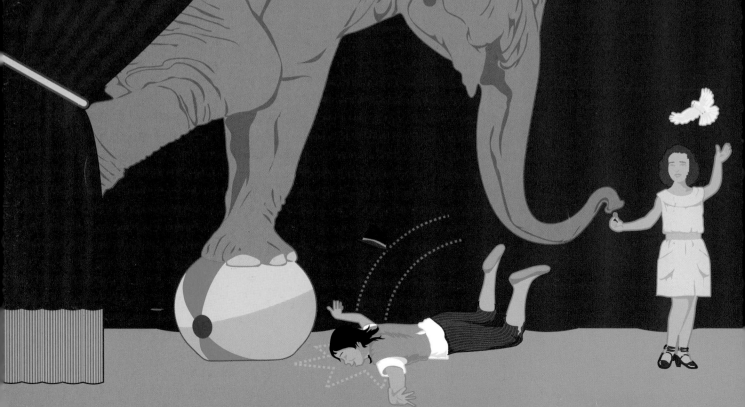

Line up a hat brim with your outstretched arm.

Flick your wrist to roll it quickly down your arm.

Dip your arm to keep up the momentum.

Catch the hat once it reaches your hand.

spin a plate ⭐ 67

1

Put a stick under a plastic plate's rim.

2

Start rotating the stick, holding the bottom still.

3

When the plate is spinning fast, hold the stick still.

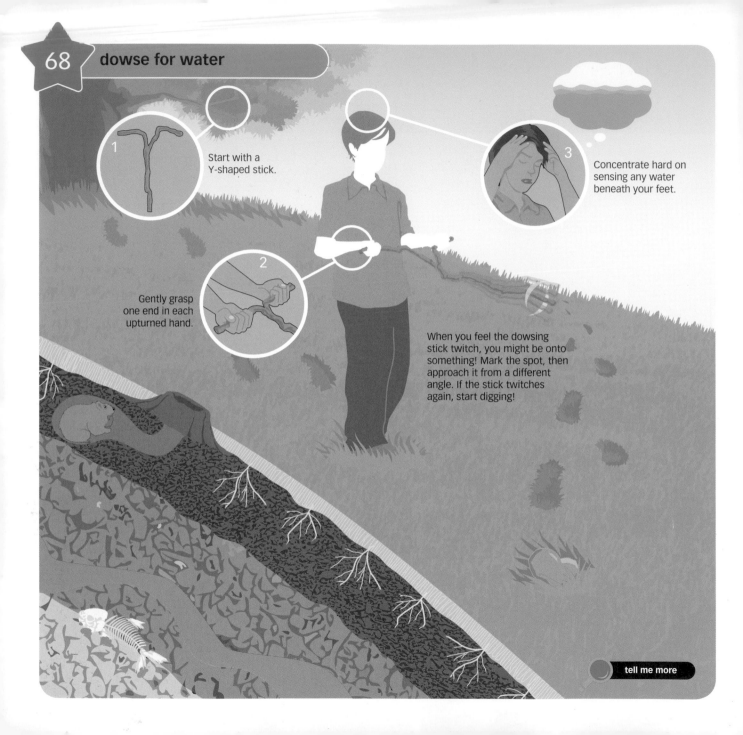

1 Start with a Y-shaped stick.

3 Concentrate hard on sensing any water beneath your feet.

2 Gently grasp one end in each upturned hand.

When you feel the dowsing stick twitch, you might be onto something! Mark the spot, then approach it from a different angle. If the stick twitches again, start digging!

tell me more

tell me more

wavy = noncommittal

broken = cloudy past

short = crushaholic

down-sloping = needy

long = romantic

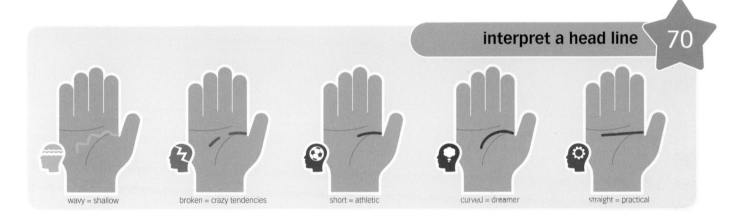

wavy = shallow

broken = crazy tendencies

short = athletic

curved = dreamer

straight = practical

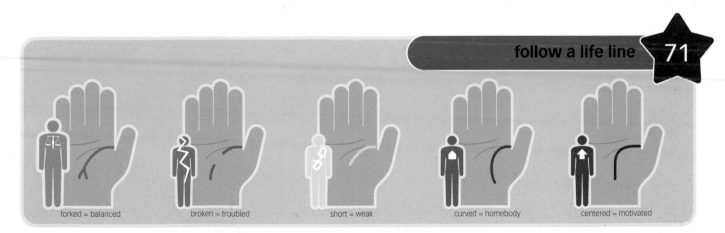

forked = balanced

broken = troubled

short = weak

curved = homebody

centered = motivated

slice an unpeeled banana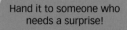

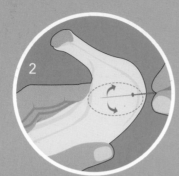

Slide the pin in a circle
inside the peel.

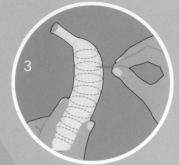

Continue slicing all the
way down the fruit.

Poke a pin into a banana
along one seam.

Hand it to someone who
needs a surprise!

Set the microwave on high for twenty seconds.

Arm each marshmallow by inserting a toothpick "spear." When the dust clears and the morphing, oozing, and melting stops, the marshmallow in better shape is the winner.

tell me more

blow a nose bubble

Chew gum until it's soft.

Stretch out the gum. Press to make an airtight seal.

Blow through your nose, holding the gum's edges.

A good bubble-blower "nose" when to stop!

If you prefer to keep your gum in your mouth, try blowing a bubble inside a bubble! Blow a big bubble, seal it shut, and use the excess gum to blow a small bubble inside it.

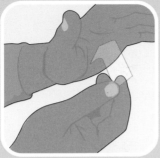

Stick one edge of a piece of tape to your palm.

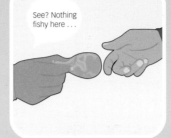

Hand the balloon to a friend for inspection.

Have him inflate it, tie it, and hand it back to you.

Attach the tape in a stealthy manner.

Press the pin into the tape—nothing happens!

Pop the balloon for a big finish.

76 walk the dog

1

Hook the loop onto
your middle finger.

2

Make a fist. Snap your
wrist down hard.

3

Gently lower
the yo-yo.

4

Stop it at the floor.

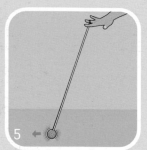

5

The yo-yo will "walk"
on its own.

6

Jerk it back up to
your hand.

77 rock the baby

1

Toss the yo-yo over
the back of your hand.

2

Lift your bottom hand
to double the string.

3

Hook the string with
your thumb.

4

Turn your top hand over
so that it's palm up.

5

Lift your bottom hand.
Pinch the string.

6

Let the baby "rock" in
the string triangle.

1

Toss one ball in half a figure eight.

2

Keep your eye on the ball!

3

Add a second ball.

4

As the first ball peaks, toss in the second.

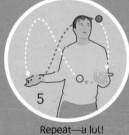

5

Repeat—a lot!

6

Get ready to add a third ball.

7

As the first ball peaks, toss in the second.

8

As the second peaks, toss in the third ball.

9

To end, catch two balls in one hand.

10

Ta-da!

How do you keep these balls—or other things—in the air? It helps to number each object as you throw it, calling out "one," "two," "three," and so on.

spin a basketball

Hold the ball with just your fingertips.

Spin it up onto one fingertip.

Balance it on your finger until it slows down.

Switch to your other hand. Brush to keep it spinning.

skip a stone

Pick a flat, smooth, rounded rock.

Curl your index finger around it.

Aim to skim the stone along the surface.

Crouch slightly, curling your arm to your body.

Space your feet widely.
Hold the ball palm-down.

Bounce the ball between
your legs. Catch.

Repeat, bouncing
from back to front.

Catch it.

Fling your arm out and
flick your wrist to release.

Watch it skip into
the sunset.

booby-trap a bathroom

Fill the showerhead with colored candy.

Fill the soap dispenser with jam.

Block part of the tap with tape.

Buy a toy spider.

Tuck the toy spider in the spigot.

Tape a plastic snake under the toilet lid.

Place bubble packaging under the toilet seat.

Tape a piece of tissue across the door. If it's broken, you'll know someone opened the door!

Tape a hair across your diary's covers.

Tape your top-secret documents inside your closet wall, just above the door.

Record intruders' handprints in flour.

Mr. Teddy's insides are a great hiding place!

Stuff helium balloons in a dresser drawer and marbles in a cabinet.

conditioner + petroleum jelly + + + plastic wrap

spirit gum

Apply petroleum jelly around your hairline.

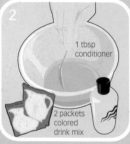

1 tbsp conditioner

2 packets colored drink mix

Make a paste from drink mix and conditioner.

Work into hair with gloved hands and a toothbrush.

Let sit under plastic.

Rinse.

Apply spirit gum to the tooth.

Spirit gum is an adhesive used by theater and movie makeup artists. You can pick some up at a drugstore.

This dye job will be subtle and should only last a few washes—unless you have blond hair. Color will be brighter and last *much* longer in light hair.

Cut out a tooth-size square of foil.

Press the foil on. Smooth out any bubbles.

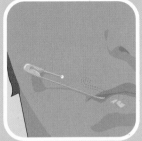

Snip the arm of a safety pin in half.

Put glue on the tip. Secure the loose end.

Bend back the very tip of the pin arm.

Now it's safe to stick the pin in your cheek.

sport spiky hair 87

hair gel   hair spray

Put gel in wet hair. Twist into spikes.

Blow-dry on warm.

Set with hair spray.

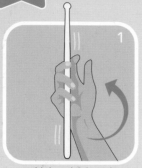

Hold the stick loosely.

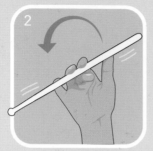

Roll it over your middle finger.

Let it roll to an upright position.

Roll it over your ring finger.

Catch it and roll it over your pinkie.

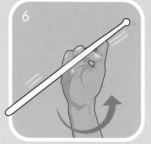

Catch it with your index finger. Repeat.

Crouch down low, then spring up.

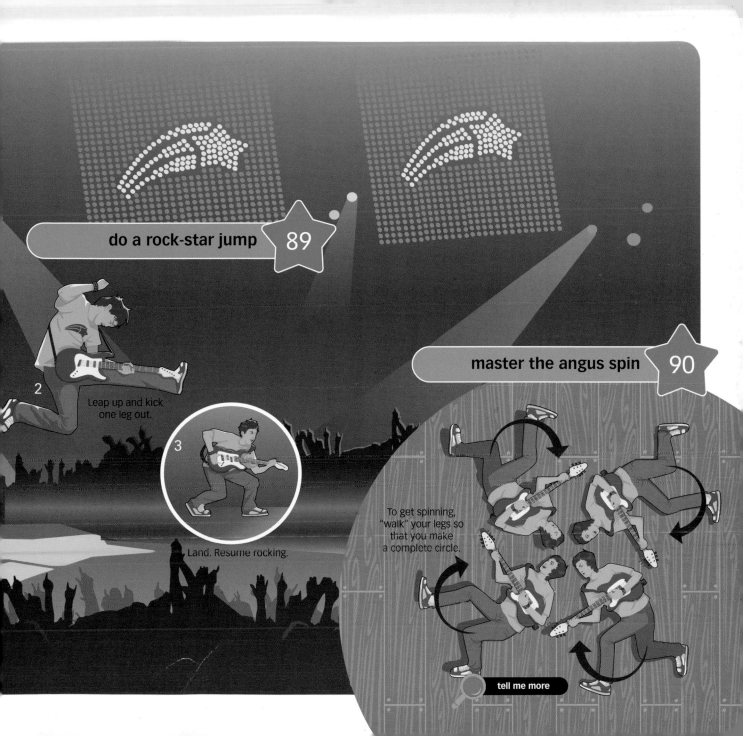

do a rock-star jump **89**

Leap up and kick one leg out.

Land. Resume rocking.

master the angus spin **90**

To get spinning, "walk" your legs so that you make a complete circle.

tell me more

tell me more

tell me more

Pssst! Want to know more about a project in this book? This handy section is full of trivia, history, and extra expert advice that will help you tackle certain activities or better understand what's so awesome about them.

39 run a ninja obstacle course

The word "ninja" is derived from a Japanese word meaning "stealthy." As you might expect, the history of these ancient, secretive, and deadly warriors is tough to pin down! In ancient Japan, both boys and girls trained to be ninjas. One favorite trick was to wear sandals with bottoms carved to look like animal prints so that the ninja could sneak around without leaving footprints.

14 set up a bocce match

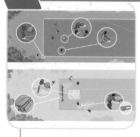

The rules shown here are from a version of the game called open bocce. Because this game has been popular all over the world since the time of the Ancient Romans, there are plenty of small, international variations. So when you travel, be sure to try *pétanque* or *boules* in France, bowls in England, *bolas criollas* in Venezuela, and *klootschieten* in the Netherlands.

47 make a floating finger

Think your eyes are playing tricks on you? You're right. As both of your eyes focus on your fingers, their paths of vision converge at one point. But then your eyes must make their paths of vision nearly parallel to focus on a distant object. While both your eyes can still see your fingertips, they see slightly overlapped images. This illusion is called a trick of perspective.

15 toss horseshoes

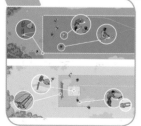

Horseshoes is another game with roots in Ancient Rome; it is probably based on the Olympic sport of discus. It was a popular pastime for soldiers during many wars, including the American Revolutionary War. When soldiers went home, horseshoes became a family game, then an official sport with famous players. Horseshoes is related to the Scottish game of quoits.

49 fake mummy organs

Before placing deceased love ones in sarcophagi, Ancient Egyptians would "mummify" them by wrapping their bodies in linen strips. They'd also remove some of the bodies' organs, which were then washed, dried, bandaged, and placed in special jars. It sure sounds like a lot of trouble, but the Egyptians believed that this process ensured a pleasant afterlife for the deceased.

hear a galloping horse 57

Before television, people listened to drama or comedy shows on the radio. To make these stories sound realistic and action-packed, radio shows hired "soundmen." These technicians used common objects to improvise noises, which brought the action of a story to life.

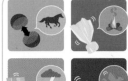

Here are a few more classic radio tricks for you to try.

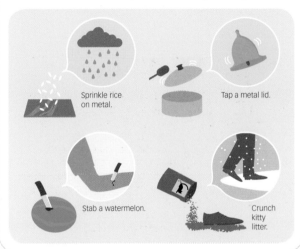

Sprinkle rice on metal.

Tap a metal lid.

Stab a watermelon.

Crunch kitty litter.

read a love line 69

To read a friend's palm, start with her dominant hand (the hand she writes with). The lines on this hand will show you behaviors and attitudes that are firmly set in this person, as well as her past actions. Next read her other hand (the passive hand). These lines will tell you her potential in the future. Remember, palm reading is just for fun—don't take it too seriously!

fight a marshmallow war 73

Can't find these exact marshmallow creatures in your local grocery store? No worries—you can make your own 'mallow monsters. Stack a few marshmallows and outfit them with cheese crackers or sandwich sticks. Then let them fight it out in the microwave.

dowse for water 68

People all around the world have practiced dowsing, also known as "water witching," for centuries. Dowsers claim to be able to locate water, oil, mineral deposits, and even lost objects using their minds—and a stick that twitches when the goods are found. Is it for real? Scientists tend to say no, but farmers and miners around the world continue to pay top dollar for dowsers' services.

master the angus spin 90

When you try this move, you may look like an idiot—but you'll be in good company! The invention of the Angus Spin is credited to vaudeville performer Curly Howard, one of the original Three Stooges. The move became a part of rock 'n' roll history when it was adopted by Angus Young of the band AC/DC (thus earning its name). Homer Simpson is another famous practitioner.

index

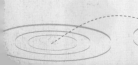

about the authors

Sarah Hines Stephens first learned to cook in order to get out of doing the dishes, and she still prefers making messes to cleaning them. One of three creative sisters, Sarah hails from generations of do-it-yourselfers: quilters, artists, writers, and gardeners. When Sarah is not facilitating semiexplosive science experiments and kid-friendly crafts, she writes books for kids. She has written more than sixty books. She lives with her husband and two children in a home filled with glitter, fabric scraps, glue, and power tools.

Bethany Mann is Sarah's sister and partner in creative mess-making. With a rallying cry of, "Hey, we could totally make that ourselves!" she has fearlessly led her family and friends in numerous craft adventures. These days Bethany channels her artistic powers for good by using recycled materials and growing vegetables. Her projects have been featured in craft books for adults and on DIY TV. She lives with her husband, teenage son, and a menagerie of rescued pets in the mountains near Santa Cruz, California. Read her blog at www.bitterbettyindustries.blogspot.com.

WELDON OWEN INC.

CEO, President Terry Newell

VP, Sales and New Business Development Amy Kaneko

VP, Publisher Roger Shaw

Creative Director Kelly Booth

Executive Editor Mariah Bear

Senior Editor Lucie Parker

Project Editor Frances Reade

Assistant Editors Emelie Griffin, Katharine Moore

Senior Designers Stephanie Tang, Meghan Hildebrand

Designer Delbarr Moradi

Illustration Coordinators Sheila Masson, Conor Buckley

Production Director Chris Hemesath

Production Manager Michelle Duggan

weldonowen

415 Jackson Street, Suite 200
San Francisco, CA 94111
Telephone: 415 291 0100
Fax: 415 291 8841
www.weldonowen.com

A division of

BONNIER

Do It Now! Tricks: Rad Stunts & Sneaky Pranks

Excerpted from **Show Off,** first published by Candlewick Press in 2009.

Library of Congress Control Number: 2012932625

ISBN 13: 978-1-61628-391-9
ISBN 10: 1-61628-391-2

10 9 8 7 6 5 4 3 2 1
2016   2015   2014   2013   2012

Printed in China by 1010 Printing International Ltd

Typeset in Vectora LH

A Show Me Now Book.
Show Me Now is a trademark
of Weldon Owen Inc.

Special thanks to:

Storyboarders

Esy Casey, Julumarie Joy Cornista, Sarah Lynn Duncan, Chris Hall, Paula Rogers, Jamie Spinello, Brandi Valenza

Illustration specialists

Hayden Foell, Raymond Larrett, Ross Sublett

Editorial and research support team

Ian Cannon, Marc Caswell, Mollie Church, Elizabeth Dougherty, Kat Engh, Alex Eros, Justin Goers, Sarah Gurman, Susan Jonaitis, Peter Masiak, Grace Newell, Jennifer Newens, Paul Ozzello, Ben Rosenberg, Hiya Swanhuyser

Kid-reviewer panel

Emma Arlen, Leah Cohen, Sally Elton, Whitman Hall, Tesserae Honor, Nami Kaneko, Emily Newell, Eloise Shaw, Georgia Shaw

Illustration credits

Front cover

Liberum Donum (Juan Calle, Santiago Calle, Andres Penagos): horseshoes Otis Thomson: go-kart Gabhor Utomo: feet Tina Cash Walsh: tire swing

Back cover

Britt Hanson: horse, marshmallow war, showerhead with paint Vic Kulihin: yo-yo, juggling Raymond Larrett: banana Liberum Donum (Juan Calle, Santiago Calle, Andres Penagos): fake wound, bocce, gymnast on high bar Christine Meighan: backward skating, scooter Gabhor

Utomo: swimmer, soccer player Tina Cash Walsh: ice rink, handstand, tire swing Mary Zins: shadow puppets

Interiors

Key: bg = background; bd = border; fr = frames; ex = extra art

Kelly Booth: 69–71 Hayden Foell: 62 bd, 63 bd, 75 bg, 77 Britt Hanson: 11 bg, 12–13, 57–60, 62–64 bg, 73, 74 bg, 82–83 Joshua Kemble: 18–19 Vic Kulihin: 38, 39, 76, 78 fr, 80 Raymond Larrett: 65–68, 72, 74 fr, 75 fr Liberum

Donum: 3 bg, 4 bg, 5 bg, 14–15, 20–21, 27–28, 32–34, 40–43, 50, 54–56, 78 ex, 79, 81 Christine Meighan: 3 fr, 4 fr, 5 fr, 44, 62 Vincent Perea: 48–49 Bryon Thompson: 6–9, 22–24, 35–36 Otis Thomson: 1–2 Gabhor Utomo: 16–17, 25–26, 46–47, 51–53, 61, 84–90 Tina Cash Walsh: 10–11 fr, 29–31, 37, 63 fr, 64 fr Mary Zins: 45